# Budgeting Basics Q&A

by

Pinnacle Press

I0465720

BUDGETING
BASICS

Q&A

PINNACLE PRESS

# Introduction

Welcome to **Budgeting Basics Q&A**, a book that makes personal finance simple, and achievable for everyone, regardless of income or financial background. If you've picked up this book, chances are you're ready to take control of your finances, reduce stress, and build a life that aligns with your goals. Whether you're new to budgeting or looking to refresh your approach, this guide will provide you with practical insights, clear strategies, and the confidence to make informed financial choices.

**Why Budgeting Matters**

Budgeting is often seen as restrictive, but it's actually the opposite, it's liberating. A budget is simply a plan that shows you where your money goes, helping you make intentional choices about how to spend, save, and invest. Imagine living a life where you aren't constantly worried about bills or debt. Picture being able to save for things that truly matter, like a home, education, or that dream vacation. With budgeting, this isn't just possible; it's entirely achievable.

**When you have a budget, you gain:**

Clarity: You know exactly where your money is going, and that knowledge allows you to manage it effectively.
Control: Instead of wondering where your money went at the end of each month, you decide in advance how it will be used.
Confidence: When you're budgeting, you can make decisions without fear. You're actively working toward financial security and independence.

**How This Book is Structured**

This book is designed to guide you through the essentials of budgeting step by step, using a question-and-answer format. Each chapter addresses a specific aspect of budgeting, from understanding income and expenses to setting goals, managing debt, and preparing for major life events. By breaking down each topic into questions, we'll approach budgeting in a way that feels natural and easy to understand. You'll find answers to common concerns, strategies to overcome challenges, and practical steps to apply to your own life.

**What You'll Learn**

Throughout this book, you'll gain tools and strategies to:

Understand Your Financial Environment: Learn the basics of tracking income and expenses and how to see the big picture of your finances.

Set and Achieve Financial Goals: Discover how to establish goals that motivate and give you more control, whether it's building an emergency fund, saving for a house, or planning for retirement.

Control Debt and Build Savings: Get practical tips on managing debt, building a savings safety net, and preparing for the future.

Adapt to Life Changes: Learn how to adjust your budget for life's surprises, from career changes to family events, so you can stay on track no matter what.

Use Technology to Make Budgeting Easier: Examine the apps and tools that simplify budgeting, allowing you to track expenses, automate savings, and stay organized.

Achieve Financial Independence: Ultimately, understand how budgeting fits into a broader journey toward financial freedom, where you have the choice to live life on your terms.

**A Realistic, Flexible Approach to Budgeting**

This book emphasizes a flexible approach to budgeting. Life is unpredictable, and rigid financial plans often lead to frustration. Instead, you'll learn how to create a budget that adapts to your circumstances and evolves with your changing needs. With a few small steps each month, budgeting can become a natural part of your life.

So, let's begin.

# Table of Contents

# Chapter 1: Introduction to Budgeting

1. What is budgeting, and why is it important?

Budgeting is a plan for managing your income and expenses. It helps you understand where your money is going and allows you to direct it toward your goals. Budgeting is important because it helps you achieve financial goals, reduces stress, and gives you control over your finances.

2. How can budgeting improve my financial health?

Budgeting can improve your financial health by reducing debt, increasing savings, and helping you make smarter financial decisions. A clear plan prevents overspending and prepares you for future expenses.

3. Is budgeting just for people with financial problems?

No, budgeting is not just for people with financial problems. It benefits anyone who wants to make the most of their income, regardless of how much they earn. Many financially successful people use budgeting to sustain their wealth.

4. Is budgeting the same as saving?

No, budgeting is not the same as saving.

5. How does budgeting differ from saving?

Budgeting is the process of planning your income and expenses, while saving is one of the results of effective budgeting. A well-structured budget helps create opportunities to save more money.

6. Can a budget be flexible?

Yes, a budget can and should be flexible. It can be adjusted to fit changing circumstances, goals, or unexpected expenses. Small tweaks can make a budget more accommodating without losing its effectiveness.

7. What are the common fears or misconceptions about budgeting?

Common fears or misconceptions about budgeting include the idea that budgeting is too restrictive or time-consuming. However, budgeting is a helpful tool, not a limitation. Start small, and it will become easier over time.

8. How much time does it take to create and maintain a budget?

Initially, setting up a budget may take a bit of time, but once it's in place, maintaining it becomes quicker. You can expect to spend some time each week reviewing and adjusting your budget.

9. Is a budget the same as a financial plan?

No, a budget is not the same as a financial plan.

10. What's the difference between a budget and a financial plan?

A budget is a short-term tool for managing monthly income and expenses, while a financial plan focuses on long-term goals like retirement or buying a home. Budgeting can be a stepping stone to a solid financial plan.

11. Do I need a budget even if I don't have much income?

Yes, you need a budget even if you don't have much income. Budgeting is valuable for everyone, especially those with lower incomes. It helps you make the most of every dollar and can lead to significant improvements in financial stability over time.

12. What should I expect when starting a budget?

When starting a budget, expect a learning curve, and understand that it's normal to find budgeting challenging at first. Focus on progress, not perfection. Small wins, like identifying overspending, can lead to bigger successes.

13. How can I make budgeting enjoyable or even fun?

You can make budgeting fun by setting up challenges, rewarding yourself for reaching milestones, or using colorful charts and apps. Also, achieving financial goals can be a great motivator.

# Chapter 2: Understanding Income and Expenses

1. What is the difference between income and expenses?

Income is the money you earn, such as wages, freelance earnings, or passive income. Expenses are the money you spend on living costs, bills, and purchases.

2. How do I calculate my total income accurately?

To calculate your total income accurately, include wages, bonuses, side jobs, and passive income. For irregular income, like freelance work, average it over time for a clearer picture.

3. What are fixed expenses?

Fixed expenses are regular, consistent costs like rent, mortgage, and car payments.

4. What are variable expenses?

Variable expenses are costs that vary monthly, like utilities, groceries, and fuel.

5. What are discretionary expenses?

Discretionary expenses are non-essential expenses like entertainment, dining out, and hobbies.

6. Why is it important to categorize your expenses?

Categorizing your expenses helps you understand where your money goes.

7. How can I track my monthly expenses without feeling overwhelmed?

To track your monthly expenses without feeling overwhelmed, use budgeting apps, keep a spending journal, or check your bank statements regularly. Start by tracking just a few categories to make the process manageable.

8. What are some common categories to include in a budget?

Common categories to include in a budget are housing, transportation, food, utilities, insurance, debt payments, savings, and entertainment. Customize these categories to suit your financial priorities and lifestyle.

9. Is it important to distinguish between needs and wants?

Yes, it is very important to distinguish between needs and wants.

10. Why is it important to distinguish between needs and wants?

Distinguishing between needs and wants helps you prioritize essential spending over discretionary purchases. Needs include housing and groceries, while wants are things like entertainment or luxury items. Focusing on needs first makes budgeting easier.

11. How do I handle irregular expenses, like car repairs or medical bills?

To handle irregular expenses effectively, set aside a portion of your income each month into a "sinking fund" for irregular expenses like car maintenance, healthcare, or annual subscriptions. This helps cover these costs without disrupting your budget.

12. What's the best way to handle cash vs. credit card spending in my budget?

Both cash and credit card spending should be tracked in your budget. Be mindful of credit card expenses to avoid debt, and consider using cash for discretionary spending to stay within limits.

13. How do I know if I'm spending too much in a particular category?

To know if you are spending too much in a particular category, set spending limits for each category based on your income and financial goals. Track your monthly spending and compare it to these limits. Adjust your budget if you consistently overspend in any area.

14. How can I adjust my budget when my income changes?

When your income changes, re-evaluate your spending priorities. You can reduce discretionary expenses or savings contributions when income decreases and increase savings or investments when income rises.

15. How do I balance multiple sources of income (e.g., salary, freelance work)?

To balance multiple sources of income, track each income source individually or combine them for simplicity. Allocate money from each source toward specific expenses or savings goals to ensure balanced financial management.

16. Should I budget based on my net or gross income?

It's more practical to budget based on your net income (post-tax), as that's the money you take home. However, understanding your gross income is helpful for long-term financial planning.

17. What are some signs of "leakage" in my spending, and how do I stop it?

Spending leaks are small, unplanned expenses like daily coffees or unused subscriptions. Track these small purchases closely, and eliminate unnecessary spending to stop the leaks.

18. What's the importance of tracking and managing both income and expenses?

Tracking both income and expenses is crucial for making informed financial decisions, gaining a clear picture of your financial health, and taking control of your financial future.

19. What is "lifestyle inflation"?

Lifestyle inflation is when you increase spending as your income increases.

20. How can I avoid "lifestyle inflation" when my income increases?

To avoid lifestyle inflation when your income increases, put raises or bonuses toward savings or debt payments, and limit lifestyle upgrades to stay on track with your financial goals.

# Chapter 3: Setting Financial Goals

1. Why is it important to set financial goals before budgeting?

Setting financial goals before budgeting gives your budget purpose by providing direction and motivation. Clear goals help you make intentional choices with your money, making it easier to stick to your budget and achieve long-term financial security.

2. What are the different types of financial goals?

The different types of financial goals are:

Short-term goals: (under 1 year) like building an emergency fund or paying off small debts.
Medium-term goals: (1–5 years) such as saving for a car, vacation, or wedding.
Long-term goals: (5+ years) including buying a house, retirement, or children's education. Balancing these goal types is key to a well-rounded financial plan.

3. How do I prioritize my financial goals?

Prioritize goals based on urgency and personal importance. Assess which goals align with your financial situation, lifestyle, and future aspirations. Often, emergency funds, debt repayment, and retirement savings take priority, but this varies for each individual.

4. How do I set realistic, achievable financial goals?

To set realistic and achievable financial goals, use the SMART framework (Specific, Measurable, Achievable, Relevant, Time-bound). For example, aim to save $500 for an emergency fund in three months. Specific, well-defined goals are easier to track and achieve.

5. What's the difference between saving goals and spending goals?

The difference between saving goals and spending goals are:

Saving goals: Focus on accumulating money (e.g., emergency fund, retirement).
Spending goals: Focus on planned purchases (e.g., vacation, big purchase).

6. How can I align my goals with my values?

To align your goals with your values, values-based budgeting connects your spending and saving habits with what matters most to you, like family, education, or health. Reflect on your core values to increase motivation and prevent unnecessary spending.

7. How do I set goals if I have debt?

To set goals if you have debt, balance debt repayment with savings goals. Pay off high-interest debt first while setting aside some money for savings, even if it's small. This prevents feeling restricted and helps you build toward future financial security.

8. What should my first financial goal be if I'm new to budgeting?

Start with a small, achievable goal, like building an emergency fund of $500–$1,000 or tracking all expenses for a month. These starter goals build confidence and set the foundation for bigger goals later.

9. How do I set goals for uncertain future expenses?

To set goals for uncertain future expenses, use "sinking funds" to save for anticipated but irregular expenses like car repairs or home maintenance. Set aside small amounts each month to cover these costs without disrupting your budget.

10. How much should I allocate to each goal?

A common rule of thumb is the 50/30/20 budget: 50% on needs, 30% on wants, and 20% on financial goals like savings, investments, or debt repayment. Adjust these percentages based on your priorities and timeline for each goal.

11. What role does an emergency fund play in my goals?

An emergency fund is a foundational goal. It acts as a safety net, preventing debt during unexpected expenses. Aim to save three to six months' worth of living expenses for peace of mind.

12. How often should I review and adjust my financial goals?

Review your financial goals at least annually or after major life changes (e.g., job change, moving). Adjust your goals to reflect current priorities or financial conditions, as goal-setting is an ongoing process.

13. How can I stay motivated when working toward long-term goals?

When working towards long-term goals, break large goals into smaller milestones and celebrate achievements along the way. Use tools like progress trackers or visualize the end result to stay motivated.

14. How can I manage multiple financial goals at once?

To manage multiple financial goals at once, use a "goal stacking" strategy by focusing on one major goal at a time while maintaining smaller contributions to secondary goals. For example, build an emergency fund first, then shift focus to debt repayment.

15. Can inflation and economic changes impact my goals?

Yes, inflation and economic changes can impact your goals.

16. What's the impact of inflation and economic changes on my goals?

Inflation reduces purchasing power, so you may need to adjust savings for long-term goals like retirement. Regularly review inflation rates and adjust your financial goals to ensure they remain achievable over time.

# Chapter 4: Building Your First Budget

1. What are the basic steps to creating a budget?

The basic steps to creating a budget are:

Identify your income.
List your expenses.
Set financial goals.
Allocate funds based on your income.
Track and adjust as needed.

Remember, budgeting is about planning and organizing, not perfection.

2. How do I choose the right budgeting method for me?

You can choose the right budgeting methods with some popular budgeting methods:

Zero-Based Budgeting: Assign every dollar to a specific category, so income minus expenses equals zero.
50/30/20 Rule: Allocate 50% to needs, 30% to wants, and 20% to financial goals.
Envelope System: Use cash for spending categories to control expenses.

Try different methods to find what works best for you.

3. What is a zero-based budget, and how does it work?

In a zero-based budget, every dollar is assigned a job, from expenses to savings. This promotes accountability by ensuring that all your income is purposefully allocated. For example, you might assign $500 to rent, $300 to food, and so on until every dollar is accounted for.

4. What is the 50/30/20 rule, and is it a good fit for beginners?

The 50/30/20 rule divides your income into 50% for needs, 30% for wants, and 20% for financial goals. It's a simple, flexible method ideal for beginners with steady income who prefer less detailed budgeting.

5. How do I determine how much to allocate to each category?

To determine how much to allocate to each category, start with a percentage-based approach, such as 30–35% for housing, 10–15% for food, and 10–20% for transportation. Adjust these based on your actual spending and needs as you track your expenses.

6. How often should I update my budget?

Review your budget monthly to see if you met your goals and adjust for the upcoming month. This routine helps you spot spending trends and build confidence in managing your finances.

7. What should I do if I consistently go over budget in certain categories?

If you consistently go over budget in certain categories, revisit your budget to see if it's realistic. Either increase the budget for that category or find ways to cut back on spending.

8. How do I budget if I have irregular income?

If you have irregular income, use a "bare-bones budget" based on your lowest expected income each month. Allocate any extra income to secondary goals or savings. This provides a safety net for months with lower earnings.

9: How do I incorporate savings and debt repayment into my budget?

To incorporate savings and debt repayment into your budget, prioritize savings and debt repayment by allocating 10–20% of your income toward these goals. Paying down debt reduces interest costs, while saving helps build financial security.

10. How do I adjust my budget for seasonal expenses?

To adjust your budget for seasonal expenses, use seasonal budgeting by setting aside funds during lower-cost months to cover higher expenses during holidays or back-to-school season. A sinking fund can help you prepare for these costs.

11. How can I manage discretionary spending without feeling restricted?

To manage discretionary spending without feeling restricted, include discretionary spending in your budget by creating a "fun fund" for entertainment or hobbies. Budgeting for wants makes the process more sustainable and enjoyable.

12. Should I use cash, credit, or debit when budgeting?

It depends:

Cash is good for controlling discretionary spending.
Credit is useful if paid in full monthly to avoid interest.
Debit directly tracks spending from your checking account.

Choose the option that aligns with your spending habits and discipline.

13. How can I make budgeting easier if I don't like numbers?

If you don't like numbers, use budgeting apps that automate calculations, or round numbers to the nearest dollar. Focus on key categories to reduce the complexity and make budgeting more approachable.

14. How much should I keep in my checking account for regular expenses?

Keep enough for a full month's expenses, plus a small buffer for unexpected costs. This helps prevent overdrafts and ensures a smoother budgeting process.

15. How can I handle unexpected expenses that come up mid-month?

To handle unexpected expenses that come up mid-month, set aside a "miscellaneous" or "buffer" fund in your budget for unplanned expenses. If this fund runs out, reallocate from other categories temporarily and replenish it next month.

16. What's the role of a "sinking fund" in a budget, and how do I create one?

A sinking fund is a savings pool for planned but irregular expenses, like car repairs or holidays. Divide the total cost by the number of months until the expense, and save that amount each month.

17: How do I know when my budget is "working'?

A successful budget helps you achieve financial goals, avoid unnecessary debt, and reduce financial stress. Track your progress, make changes as needed, and remember that flexibility is key to a well-functioning budget.

# Chapter 5: Tracking and Managing Your Budget

1. Why is tracking my spending important once I have a budget?

Tracking your spending helps ensure you stay within your budget and reveals areas where adjustments may be needed. It provides insights into your spending habits, reinforces accountability, and prevents overspending.

2. How do I track my spending without feeling overwhelmed?

Start with simple methods like using a budgeting app, keeping a spending diary, or reviewing bank statements weekly. Begin by tracking a few key categories before expanding to everything to ease into the habit.

3. What are the best tools for tracking my budget?

The best tools for tracking your budget include:

Apps: Mint, YNAB (You Need a Budget), PocketGuard, etc.
Spreadsheets: Google Sheets, Microsoft Excel with budget templates.
Manual: Pen-and-paper budget journals.

Try different tools to see which one works best for your needs.

4. How often should I check my spending?

A weekly check-in is ideal to monitor spending and make changes. Do a monthly review to assess the big picture and see if any changes are needed for the next month.

5. What should I do if I exceed my budget in a category?

If you exceed a budget in a category, avoid guilt and analyze why you went over. Reallocate funds from other categories or adjust your budget for the next month. This is a learning opportunity to align your budget more closely with real expenses.

6. How do I handle unexpected expenses that disrupt my budget?

Use an emergency fund for major unexpected expenses and a small buffer fund for minor surprises. Adjust other categories temporarily to cover the cost, then work to rebuild the buffer over time.

7. How can I prevent impulse spending from derailing my budget?

To prevent impulse spending from derailing your budget, use strategies like a 24-hour waiting period for unplanned purchases, set spending limits for non-essential items, or create a "wish list" for future buys. Delaying purchases helps you avoid regret and stick to your budget.

8. How can I stay motivated to track my budget consistently?

To stay motivated to track your budget consistently, set small rewards for staying within budget and celebrate financial wins like paying off debt or hitting savings goals. Use visual aids like progress bars or charts to make your progress more satisfying.

9. What are some common budgeting pitfalls to watch out for?

Common pitfalls include underestimating variable expenses, forgetting seasonal costs, and not adjusting the budget when income or expenses change. Stay mindful of these to avoid frustration and build a realistic budget.

10. How do I track cash expenses without losing track?

To track cash expenses without losing track, set aside a fixed cash amount for spending categories like groceries or dining out and keep receipts. Enter cash expenses into your tracking tool weekly or use an envelope system for easy monitoring.

11. How do I handle a budget surplus at the end of the month?

To handle a budget surplus at the end of each month, allocate surpluses toward financial goals like paying extra on debt, adding to savings, or contributing to a sinking fund. You can also keep a small reward for yourself to stay motivated.

12. How can I manage my budget if I share expenses with a partner or roommate?

If you share expenses with a partner or roommate, open communication is key. Use a shared budgeting tool or app (e.g., Splitwise) to manage joint expenses like rent or utilities. Regular check-ins can help align financial goals and ensure expenses are covered.

13. How do I account for spending habits that vary from month to month?

To account for spending habits that vary from month to month, use "rolling" categories, where unspent funds in one month carry over to the next. For variable expenses like utilities, set an average amount based on previous months and adjust as needed.

14. How can I make tracking expenses part of my routine?

To make tracking expenses part of your routine, designate a specific day each week, such as "Money Mondays," to review and record expenses. Turning tracking into a habit makes it less of a chore and integrates it into your regular routine.

15. What's the difference between a spending tracker and a budget, and do I need both?

A budget is a plan for how you intend to spend money, while a spending tracker records what actually happens. Both are needed to compare your planned budget against actual spending and implement changes if necessary.

16. How do I know when to adjust my budget?

Adjust your budget when there's a life change (e.g., a raise or new expense) or during regular monthly reviews. Flexibility and adapting your budget to reflect current circumstances are key to its long-term success.

17. What is the "80/20 rule" in budgeting, and how does it apply to tracking?

The 80/20 rule suggests that focusing on the top 20% of spending categories can lead to 80% of the results. Concentrate on tracking your highest expenses. such as housing, food, and transportation, if tracking every small expense feels overwhelming.

# Chapter 6: Reducing Expenses and Cutting Costs

1. What are some common areas where people overspend?

Common areas where people overspend include dining out, entertainment, grocery shopping, subscription services, and impulse purchases.

2. How can I save on groceries without compromising on quality?

You can save on groceries without compromising on quality by meal planning, making a shopping list, buying in bulk, and opting for store brands. Avoid shopping when hungry, and use cashback apps or reward programs to cut costs on essentials.

3. What are some strategies for reducing utility bills?

You can lower utility bills by reducing thermostat settings, unplugging unused electronics, using energy-efficient light bulbs, and washing clothes in cold water. Small changes can lead to big savings over time.

4. How do I reduce transportation costs?

Save on transportation by carpooling, using public transportation, combining errands to save gas, and maintaining your vehicle to prevent costly repairs. For short trips, consider biking or walking to save fuel and improve health.

5. How can I cut back on dining out without feeling deprived?

Set a dining-out limit, cook more meals at home, and try a "dining out budget" or "fun fund." Make dining out an occasional treat and research meal-prep ideas to make home cooking easier and more convenient.

6. How do I manage subscriptions and memberships I'm no longer using?

Review subscriptions quarterly and cancel those you no longer use. Apps that track subscriptions or reminders for renewal dates can help avoid unwanted charges and manage recurring expenses effectively.

7. How can I control online shopping and impulse purchases?

Use a 24-hour waiting period before buying non-essential items online. Use price-tracking browser extensions and create a list of needs vs. wants before shopping to avoid impulse purchases.

8. What are some ways to reduce housing expenses?

Renters can negotiate rent or find roommates, while homeowners can refinance or downsize to save money. Energy-efficient home upgrades and checking for tax breaks can also help lower housing costs.

9. How can I enjoy entertainment without overspending?

To enjoy entertainment without overspending, look for free community events, use public parks, borrow movies and books from the library, or use streaming services. Budget-friendly activities like game nights or DIY movie nights at home can also be fun.

10. What's the best way to manage and reduce debt payments?

To manage and reduce debt payments, use the snowball or avalanche method to prioritize high-interest debt. Look for balance transfer offers, negotiate lower interest rates, or consolidate debt to reduce monthly payments.

11. How do I cut costs on insurance without sacrificing coverage?

To cut costs on insurance without sacrificing coverage, shop around for insurance annually, bundle policies, increase deductibles, or ask about discounts. Maintaining a good credit score can also lower premiums.

12. How can I save money on clothing and personal items?

To save money on clothing and personal items, shop during sales, buy second-hand, and invest in quality basics over trendy items. Consider a "one in, one out" policy to limit clothing purchases, and rent for one-time events.

13. How do I avoid lifestyle inflation as my income increases?

You can avoid lifestyle inflation by directing raises or bonuses toward savings or debt repayment, instead of increasing non-essential spending. Stick to your budget, even with higher income, to stay on track with your financial goals.

14. What is a "no-spend challenge," and how can it help me save?

A "no-spend challenge" involves committing to only buying essentials for a set period (day, week, or month). It builds awareness of spending habits and can result in significant savings by curbing impulse purchases.

15. How can I balance cutting costs without feeling deprived?

You can balance cutting costs without feeling deprived by allowing for small indulgences. Set aside a "fun" category in your budget, focus on mindful spending, and prioritize what truly brings you joy without overextending your finances.

16. What should I do with the money I save from cutting expenses?

You can redirect savings toward financial goals like building an emergency fund, increasing retirement contributions, or paying off debt faster. This boosts motivation to continue cutting unnecessary costs.

17. How do I know if I'm cutting costs in the right areas?

To know if you are cutting costs in the right areas, analyze spending trends over a few months and identify areas causing financial strain. Prioritize cutting costs in non-essential categories, making sure not to compromise your quality of life or essential needs.

# Chapter 7: Budgeting for Debt Repayment

1. Why is it important to prioritize debt repayment in my budget?

Prioritizing debt repayment is crucial because interest increases the overall cost of borrowing, making it harder to reach financial goals. Reducing or eliminating debt brings peace of mind and financial freedom.

2. How do I determine which debts to pay off first?

To determine which debts to pay off first try these two strategies:

Debt Snowball Method: Pay off the smallest debts first to gain momentum and motivation.
Debt Avalanche Method: Focus on paying off the highest-interest debts to save the most on interest.

Choose the method that fits your financial situation and personal preferences.

3. What's the difference between "good" debt and "bad" debt?

Good debt: Increases value or wealth over time (e.g., mortgages or student loans).
Bad debt: High-interest consumer debt (e.g., credit cards or payday loans) that doesn't provide long-term value.

Paying off high-interest debt should be a priority.

4. How much of my income should I allocate to debt repayment?

Aim to dedicate at least 15–20% of your income to debt repayment, especially for high-interest debts. Adjust the percentage based on your financial goals and flexibility.

5. How do I balance debt repayment with saving?

To balance debt repayment with saving, start by building a small emergency fund ($500–$1,000) to handle unexpected expenses. After that, focus on paying down debt while contributing modestly to savings to avoid going back into debt.

6. How can I negotiate with creditors to lower my debt payments?

You can negotiate lower interest rates, request fee waivers, or set up a payment plan by contacting creditors directly. Credit counseling agencies can also help if needed.

7. Should I consider debt consolidation?

It depends. Debt consolidation combines multiple debts into one payment, often at a lower interest rate. It's helpful for high-interest credit card debt. Compare consolidation options to ensure they offer savings.

8. What is a balance transfer, and how can it help with debt?

A balance transfer moves high-interest credit card debt to a new card with a lower or 0% interest rate. Make sure to pay off the balance before the promotional period ends to avoid interest.

9. How do I avoid taking on more debt while repaying existing debt?

To avoid taking on more debt while repaying existing debt, create a realistic budget with a small buffer for unexpected expenses. Build an emergency fund to avoid relying on credit cards for unplanned costs.

10. How can I stay motivated while paying off debt?

To stay motivated while paying off debt, set small goals, like paying off $500 at a time, and celebrate milestones. Visualize the benefits of a debt-free life and track your progress to stay motivated.

11. What are some common mistakes to avoid when paying down debt?

Common mistakes include ignoring high-interest debt, not budgeting for irregular expenses, and stopping retirement contributions. Focus on high-interest debt first and maintain a balanced financial approach.

12. How can I handle student loan debt within my budget?

To handle student loan debt within your budget, make use of income-driven repayment plans or refinancing for better rates. Make student loan payments a fixed part of your budget, and check if your employer offers student loan assistance.

13. Should I pay off my mortgage early?

Early mortgage payoff saves interest but may reduce cash flow for other goals. Weigh your financial goals, interest rates, and any potential tax benefits before deciding.

14. What's the benefit of automating my debt payments?

Automating payments prevents missed payments, which can result in fees and damage credit scores. Some lenders offer interest rate reductions for automatic payments, saving you money.

15. How do I budget for debt if I have irregular income?

If you have irregular income, create a "bare-bones" budget based on your lowest expected income, prioritize minimum debt payments, and apply extra funds toward debt during high-income months. Build a buffer fund during better-earning periods.

16. Can I use my tax refund or bonuses to pay down debt?

Yes, use extra income like tax refunds or bonuses to make additional debt payments. These lump-sum contributions can reduce interest and shorten your repayment timeline.

17. What should I do once I pay off my debt?

Once you pay off debt, celebrate your achievement! Redirect the money that was going toward debt into savings, investments, or other financial goals. Continue budgeting and saving to maintain a debt-free lifestyle.

# Chapter 8: Saving and Emergency Funds

1. Why is an emergency fund important?

An emergency fund is important because it provides a financial cushion for unexpected expenses, such as medical bills, car repairs, or job loss. It helps you avoid relying on credit cards or loans during emergencies, protecting your financial stability.

2. How much should I have in my emergency fund?

Start with a small emergency fund of $500–$1,000 for immediate security, then work toward saving three to six months' worth of living expenses. The ideal amount may vary depending on income stability, family size, and personal needs.

3. How do I start saving if I have a limited income?

If you have limited income, start by saving small amounts, even just a few dollars a week, to build the habit. Set up automatic transfers to a savings account and gradually increase contributions as your income grows. Consistency, even with small amounts, adds up over time.

4. How can I prioritize saving when I also have debt?

To prioritize savings even when you have debt, build a small emergency fund before aggressively paying off debt. This ensures you're prepared for unexpected expenses and don't add to your debt.

5. What's the difference between a short-term and long-term savings goal?

Short-term savings goals are achievable within a year (e.g., holiday expenses, minor repairs), while long-term goals take more time (e.g., down payment on a home, retirement). Balancing both types of goals is important for financial planning.

### 6. What are sinking funds, and how do they help with savings?

Sinking funds are designated savings for specific expenses, like a vacation or a new appliance, allowing you to save gradually and avoid debt. Divide the total amount needed by the months remaining and save that amount each month.

### 7. Should I keep my emergency fund in a separate account?

Yes, keeping your emergency fund in a separate, easily accessible account helps reduce the temptation to use it for non-emergencies. A high-yield savings account is a good option to earn interest while keeping funds liquid.

### 8. How much of my income should go toward savings each month?

Aim to save at least 10–20% of your income each month. This amount can be divided between short-term savings, emergency funds, and long-term goals, depending on your priorities and financial situation.

### 9. How can I make saving a habit?

To make saving a habit, automate savings contributions each payday to make the process effortless. Start with small, manageable amounts and gradually increase as saving becomes a routine.

### 10. Should I adjust my emergency fund as my income changes?

Yes, adjust your emergency fund to reflect changes in living expenses or income stability. Review it annually to ensure it meets your current needs, and increase the fund if your expenses or risks grow.

### 11. How do I save for irregular expenses, like holiday gifts or insurance premiums?

To save for irregular expenses, set up a sinking fund for irregular expenses by estimating the total cost, dividing by the months left before the expense, and saving that amount monthly. Planning ahead reduces financial strain.

12. How can I stay motivated to save over the long term?

To stay motivated to save over the long term, set clear, specific goals and track your progress visually, such as using a savings chart. Celebrate milestones to keep yourself motivated and remind yourself of the benefits of reaching your savings goals.

13. How should I prioritize retirement savings?

Start saving for retirement as early as possible, even if it's a small amount. Take advantage of compound interest and employer-matching contributions if available to grow your retirement savings over time.

14. Where should I keep my short-term vs. long-term savings?

Keep short-term savings in easily accessible accounts, like high-yield savings accounts, and long-term savings in investment accounts or retirement plans, which are less liquid but grow more over time.

15. How do I handle saving when faced with financial setbacks?

When faced with financial setbacks, maintain a positive mindset and, if necessary, pause or reduce savings contributions temporarily. Saving is flexible, and small amounts still matter. Resume saving as soon as your financial situation allows.

16. What are the benefits of saving for future goals vs. relying on credit?

Saving allows you to avoid interest charges and reduces financial stress. Relying on credit increases overall costs and debt. Saving for purchases promotes better financial habits and control.

17. How do I know if I'm saving enough?

Compare your savings habits to your financial goals, like retirement plans and upcoming large expenses. Conduct annual reviews to ensure your savings levels align with your future needs and lifestyle goals.

# Chapter 9: Budgeting for Major Life Events

1. How do I budget for a wedding or large celebration?

Start by setting a realistic budget and estimating costs for each aspect (venue, catering, etc.). Prioritize based on personal values, create a savings timeline, and consider DIY options or choosing off-peak dates to reduce expenses.

2. What are the first steps to budgeting for a house purchase?

Begin with a detailed savings plan for a down payment, closing costs, and moving expenses. Understand mortgage affordability, calculate possible monthly payments, and factor in ongoing maintenance costs when planning.

3. How should I prepare financially for having children?

To prepare financially for having children, plan for expected costs, such as healthcare, childcare, and baby essentials. Set up a savings fund in advance, review health insurance options, and adjust your budget to accommodate ongoing child-related expenses.

4. How do I budget for a career change or job loss?

Build an emergency fund covering six to twelve months of expenses. Temporarily reduce discretionary spending, take a look at side income sources, and create a backup plan to minimize financial disruption during the transition.

5. What steps should I take to budget for retirement?

Start early and contribute consistently to retirement accounts. Calculate retirement needs based on your desired lifestyle and consider consulting a financial advisor for a personalized retirement plan

6. How do I plan for future education expenses for myself or my children?

Use education savings accounts which offer tax benefits. Set up a dedicated education fund and contribute regularly to reduce the financial burden when education expenses arise.

7. How do I save for travel or a major vacation?

Create a travel fund, research costs, and set monthly savings goals. Book accommodations and flights in advance, and track expenses to avoid overspending during your vacation.

8. How can I budget for home renovations or improvements?

Set up a home improvement fund and research the average costs of your desired projects. Get multiple quotes, consider DIY for smaller tasks, and prioritize renovations based on necessity and available budget.

9. What's the best way to handle medical expenses and healthcare planning?

Review your health insurance to ensure adequate coverage and set up a health savings account if available. Budget for routine care and unexpected medical expenses to avoid financial strain.

10. How do I budget for my child's education from an early age?

Start saving early to make contributions manageable. Open a dedicated savings account and contribute monthly to build a fund for future educational needs.

11. How should I prepare for large purchases, like a car?

For a car, save for a down payment and research financing options to find the best rates. Budget for monthly payments, insurance, and maintenance, and weigh the pros and cons of buying new versus used.

12. How can I prepare for caregiving responsibilities for family members?

Budget for potential costs such as medical care, transportation, and home modifications. Research assistance programs and review insurance coverage to prepare for caregiving responsibilities.

13. How do I budget for relocating or moving to a new city?

To budget for relocating or moving to a new city, estimate moving costs, including transportation, deposits, and temporary housing. Create a relocation fund in advance and research the cost of living in your new city to adjust your budget accordingly.

14. How do I manage the financial impact of divorce or separation?

To manage the financial impact of divorce or separation, set up a separate emergency fund and consult a financial planner. Budget for legal fees, adjust living arrangements, and reassess your financial goals and plans post-divorce.

15. How can I prepare financially for aging parents and potential eldercare?

To prepare financially for aging parents and potential eldercare, have open discussions with family members about future needs. Set aside a fund for eldercare expenses, review insurance policies, and examine government programs that may assist with eldercare costs.

16. How do I prepare for unexpected major life events?

To prepare for unexpected major life events, maintain a robust emergency fund and keep insurance policies up to date. Regularly review your budget and savings to ensure you are prepared for sudden life changes.

17. What role does life insurance play in planning for major life events?

Life insurance provides financial security for loved ones in case of an unexpected death. Assess your insurance needs, especially during major life changes like marriage, having children, or buying a home.

# Chapter 10: Budgeting for Financial Independence

1. What is financial independence, and why should I consider it a goal?

Financial independence means being able to cover all your living expenses with passive income or savings, allowing you to work by choice rather than necessity. It provides freedom, security, and flexibility to pursue personal interests without relying on a paycheck.

2. How can budgeting help me reach financial independence?

Budgeting helps you direct funds toward savings and investments. By controlling expenses and maximizing savings, you consistently build wealth over time, which is essential for achieving financial independence.

3. What is my "freedom number," and how do I calculate it?

Your "freedom number" is the amount of money you need to cover annual expenses without working. Calculate it by multiplying your annual expenses by a retirement multiplier (typically 25 for a 4% withdrawal rate). This tells you how much you need to save to reach financial independence.

4. How much should I be saving each month to achieve financial independence?

Aim to save 20–50% of your income, depending on your goals and timeline. Saving aggressively shortens the time needed to reach financial independence, while a more moderate savings rate allows for a gradual approach.

5. How do investments contribute to financial independence?

Investments allow your wealth to grow through compound interest, helping you reach financial independence faster than saving alone. Low-cost, diversified investments like index funds or ETFs are ideal for long-term growth.

6. What's the difference between passive income and active income, and why is passive income important?

Passive income is earned with minimal ongoing effort (e.g., dividends, rental income). Active income requires time and effort (e.g., salary, freelancing). Passive income is crucial for financial independence because it generates income without active work.

7. What types of passive income can help me achieve financial independence?

Common sources of passive income include dividends from investments, rental property income, royalties, and business investments can help you achieve financial independence. Each source carries different levels of risk and involvement, so choose what fits your goals.

8. How can I make saving and investing a priority in my budget?

To make saving and investing a priority in your budget, set up automatic contributions to investment accounts and treat them like non-negotiable expenses. This "pay yourself first" approach helps you prioritize saving and reduces unnecessary spending.

9. How do I balance my current lifestyle with my future financial independence goals?

Find a balance by budgeting for discretionary spending while maintaining a savings rate high enough to stay on track for financial independence. Enjoy life now, but keep future goals in mind.

10. What role does frugality play in achieving financial independence?

Frugality reduces expenses, allowing for a higher savings rate and speeding up the path to financial independence. Small lifestyle adjustments, like minimizing unnecessary purchases, contribute to long-term savings.

11. Should I pay off all debt before pursuing financial independence?

Prioritize paying off high-interest debt first, as it can slow your progress. Low-interest debt, like a mortgage, may be managed alongside investing if the return on investments exceeds the interest rate on the debt.

12. How can I plan for healthcare costs in financial independence?

To plan for healthcare costs in financial independence, consider health savings accounts and early retirement health insurance options. Include healthcare costs in your "freedom number" to ensure your plan covers routine care and unexpected medical expenses.

13. What's the importance of regularly reviewing my financial independence plan?

Regular reviews (annually or semi-annually) of your financial independence plan help you adjust to changes in income, expenses, or goals. Flexibility allows you to stay on track despite life changes or market fluctuations.

16. How do I know if I'm on track to reach financial independence?

To know if you are on track to reach financial independence, track your net worth, investment growth, and savings rate. Use online calculators or financial planning tools to project your timeline and assess your progress toward financial independence.

17. What should I do once I achieve financial independence?

Once you achieve financial independence, continue managing your finances responsibly to sustain your independence and enjoy the freedom you've earned.

# Chapter 11: Overcoming Common Budgeting Challenges

1. What are common struggles to stick to a budget, and how can I avoid this?

Common struggles include setting unrealistic expectations, feeling restricted, or failing to review the budget regularly. To avoid these, set realistic goals, allow flexibility, and view the budget as a living document that can adapt to changing needs.

2. What should I do if my income is inconsistent?

If your income is inconsistent, create a "bare-bones budget" based on your lowest expected monthly income, focusing on essential expenses. During high-income months. build a buffer fund to cover shortfalls in leaner times and provide stability despite income fluctuations.

3. How can I stay motivated to budget when progress feels slow?

To stay motivated to budget when progress feels slow, set small, achievable milestones and celebrate each one. Track progress visually with charts or graphs and remind yourself of the long-term benefits, like achieving financial independence or reaching major life goals.

4. How do I handle a budgeting setback, like an unexpected expense or job loss?

Focus on essentials and temporarily pause non-urgent financial goals. Use an emergency fund if needed and adjust your budget to handle the setback. Gradually resume savings and debt payments as your situation improves.

5. How do I handle budgeting with a partner who has different spending habits?

Openly communicate about shared financial goals, values, and priorities. Set joint budget categories and individual "no-questions-asked" spending limits. Compromise and clearly divide financial responsibilities to encourage teamwork.

6. What if my friends and family pressure me to spend outside my budget?

Set boundaries by suggesting budget-friendly alternatives for social activities and politely explain your financial goals. Focus on your priorities and remind yourself that sticking to your budget contributes to long-term financial stability.

7. How can I avoid "budget burnout"?

To avoid "budget burnout", keep your budget flexible, allowing for occasional "treat yourself" moments and fun funds for guilt-free spending. Regularly revisit and adjust the budget to keep it engaging and aligned with your current interests and goals.

8. How do I overcome the guilt or shame of past financial mistakes?

To overcome the guilt or shame of past financial mistakes, view financial setbacks as learning experiences, not as defining moments. Focus on current progress, set achievable goals, and celebrate small wins. Remember that budgeting is about moving forward, not dwelling on the past.

9. How do I handle budgeting during inflation or rising costs?

To handle budgeting during inflation or rising costs, adjust spending limits for essential categories like groceries and utilities based on actual expenses. Cut costs in discretionary areas to make room for increased costs in necessary categories while still staying on budget.

10. How can I budget for irregular expenses that don't fit into monthly categories?

To budget for irregular expenses that don't fit into monthly categories, use sinking funds, where you save a small amount monthly for irregular expenses like car repairs or insurance premiums. Sinking funds spread the cost over the year, reducing financial strain when these expenses arise.

11. How can I budget effectively if I have trouble keeping track of receipts and expenses?

Use budgeting apps that automatically track expenses or schedule a weekly review of bank statements. Organize receipts in a folder or envelope, or use digital tools to capture receipts immediately after purchases.

12. What can I do if I consistently overspend in certain budget categories?

If you consistently overspend in certain budget categories, analyze spending patterns and set realistic limits. Find alternatives, like meal prepping instead of dining out, and adjust your budget to reflect actual habits rather than ideal goals.

13. How can I stay disciplined when budgeting feels restrictive?

When budgeting feels restrictive, re-frame your budget as a tool for freedom, as it enables you to spend intentionally and reach your goals. Allow room for discretionary spending and stay focused on the bigger picture of financial security and independence.

14. How do I handle budgeting with large amounts of debt?

If you have large amounts of debt, take a balanced approach, allocating most of your funds toward debt repayment while setting aside savings to avoid new debt. Break debt repayment into smaller, manageable steps and celebrate each victory along the way.

15. What should I do if my financial goals change?

Financial goals are flexible and can be adjusted as your priorities change. Revisit your budget periodically, especially after life changes, and make changes to reflect your new goals and circumstances.

16. How do I handle budgeting if I experience a sudden increase in income?

Plan ahead by setting new savings and investment targets before your income increases. Avoid lifestyle inflation by maintaining your current lifestyle and using extra income to reach financial goals faster.

17. How can I keep budgeting interesting and avoid getting bored?

To keep budgeting interesting and avoid getting bored, set small challenges like "no-spend days" or monthly savings goals to stay engaged. Use budgeting apps with fun features, visualize progress toward your goals, and revisit goals periodically to keep them fresh and motivating.

# Chapter 12: Using Technology to Enhance Your Budget

1. How can budgeting apps help me manage my finances?

Budgeting apps simplify managing finances by tracking expenses, setting goals, and monitoring progress. They automatically categorize spending, provide alerts for overspending, and offer visual tools like charts, making budgeting more engaging and efficient.

2. How does automation improve budgeting?

Automation streamlines budgeting by scheduling savings, bill payments, and debt repayments. It ensures that important transactions occur automatically, reducing the mental load and helping you stay consistent with your financial goals.

3. What is a financial dashboard, and how can I use it for budgeting?

A financial dashboard is a tool that centralizes all your accounts, assets, and expenses in one place. It offers a clear, quick overview of your finances, helping you make informed spending and saving decisions.

4. Can I use technology to set and track my financial goals?

Yes, apps and online tools often include goal-setting features like visual trackers or progress bars. These tools help track your progress toward financial goals, keeping you motivated as you see incremental progress over time.

5. How do budgeting apps categorize expenses, and can I customize them?

Most apps automatically categorize expenses based on spending patterns and merchant information. You can usually customize these categories to better align with your personal spending habits, providing a clearer picture of your finances.

6. How can technology help me track multiple sources of income?

Budgeting apps and spreadsheets can handle multiple income streams, from salaries to freelance work. Some apps automatically detect deposits, allowing you to see your total income and budget accordingly.

7. What are the benefits of using spreadsheets for budgeting?

Spreadsheets, like Excel or Google Sheets, offer flexibility for creating a custom budget system. They allow for personalized formatting, formulas, and charts, making them ideal for those who prefer a hands-on, highly tailored budgeting approach.

8. How can technology help me find areas to cut costs?

Expense-tracking features in apps reveal spending patterns, helping identify areas where you can cut back. Some apps also provide suggestions, such as negotiating bills or switching providers, based on your spending habits.

9. How can I protect my financial information when using apps and online tools?

To protect your financial information when using apps and online tools, use reputable apps with secure encryption, two-factor authentication, and strong privacy policies. Regularly monitor your accounts and avoid accessing financial information over public Wi-Fi to protect your data.

10. How can I use technology to stay on top of bills and avoid late fees?

To stay on top of bills and avoid late fees using technology, set up automatic payments through your bank or use bill-pay services. Budgeting apps often provide bill reminders to help you avoid late payments and associated fees, ensuring your finances stay on track.

11. How do financial calculators and tools help with budgeting?

Financial calculators for loan payoff, investment growth, and retirement planning assist in making informed decisions. Tools like mortgage or debt payoff calculators show the impact of extra payments, helping you better plan for future goals.

12. Can I use technology to stay motivated with budgeting?

Yes. Apps with goal-tracking features and visual progress updates keep budgeting engaging. Gamification elements, such as badges or streaks, can provide a sense of reward and motivation for sticking to your budget.

13. How can I avoid technology overwhelm when budgeting?

Start with one app or tool to prevent overload. Choose technology that complements your lifestyle and is easy to use consistently. The best tool is the one that helps you stay on track without adding unnecessary complexity.

# Chapter 13: Advanced Budgeting Tips and Tricks

1. What does it mean to "optimize" my budget?

Budget optimization involves refining your spending, increasing savings, and finding efficiencies in your financial plan. It's about aligning your spending with personal values, eliminating unnecessary expenses, and ensuring every dollar is working toward your financial goals.

2. How can I use the "pay yourself first" strategy to boost savings?

"Pay yourself first" means prioritizing savings and investments before other expenses. Automate transfers to savings or investment accounts immediately after receiving your paycheck, ensuring that saving becomes a consistent habit.

3. How can I implement the cash envelope system for better spending control?

The cash envelope system involves allocating cash for specific budget categories (e.g., groceries, entertainment). Once the cash in an envelope is used up, you stop spending in that category for the month. This method helps build discipline and avoid overspending.

4. What is the 80/20 budget rule, and how does it work?

The 80/20 rule allocates 80% of your income for spending (needs and wants) and 20% for savings or debt repayment. It simplifies budgeting by ensuring you consistently save while allowing flexibility for spending.

5. How can I use sinking funds to plan for future expenses more effectively?

Sinking funds are savings set aside for predictable but irregular expenses, such as vacations or car repairs. By dividing these expenses into monthly contributions, you can spread out the financial burden, making large costs more manageable.

6. What is a "bare-bones budget," and when should I use it?

A bare-bones budget covers only essential expenses, such as rent, utilities, and groceries. It's useful during financial setbacks or when aggressively saving for a goal. Having a bare-bones budget as a backup ensures you're prepared for emergencies or unexpected changes in income.

7. How can I use the "30-day rule" to avoid impulse purchases?

The 30-day rule involves waiting 30 days before making a non-essential purchase. This delay gives you time to consider whether the item fits into your budget and aligns with your financial goals, helping prevent impulsive spending.

8: How can I automate my finances to save time and improve consistency?

To automate your finances to save time and improve consistency, automate bill payments, savings contributions, and debt repayments to ensure they occur on time and consistently. Automation reduces the risk of missed payments and makes it easier to maintain financial discipline.

9. How do I budget for annual or seasonal expenses without disrupting my monthly budget?

Use sinking funds or set aside a small amount each month to cover annual or seasonal expenses like insurance premiums, holidays, or school supplies. Planning ahead spreads the cost over time and prevents budget strain.

10. What are some tax-saving strategies I can incorporate into my budget?

Use tax-advantaged accounts and health savings accounts to lower taxable income. Track deductible expenses and consult tax software or professionals to identify opportunities to maximize tax savings.

11. How can I manage lifestyle inflation as my income grows?

To manage lifestyle inflation as your income grows, allocate a portion of any raise or bonus to savings or investments. Maintain a modest lifestyle, allowing your increased income to work toward long-term financial goals rather than inflating your expenses.

12. What is the "reverse budget," and how does it differ from traditional budgeting?

In reverse budgeting, you prioritize savings and investment goals first, then allocate the remainder for expenses. This method ensures that financial goals come first and encourages living within what's left after saving.

13. What is net worth?

Net worth is the difference between your assets (what you own) and liabilities (what you owe).

14. How can I use financial ratios to assess my budget's health?

Financial ratios, like the debt-to-income ratio or savings rate, help evaluate your financial stability. These ratios provide insight into debt levels, savings adequacy, and overall resilience, guiding adjustments to your budget.

15. How do I maximize rewards and cashback programs without overspending?

Use rewards or cashback programs for planned, budgeted purchases. Pay off credit card balances each month to avoid interest and use rewards for categories you regularly spend on, such as groceries or gas.

16. How can I make investing a priority within my budget?

Set a specific percentage of your income for investments and automate contributions to retirement or brokerage accounts. Even small, regular investments grow over time through compound interest, helping you reach long-term financial goals.

17. How can I continuously improve and refine my budget over time?

Review and adjust your budget regularly, analyzing spending patterns and reassessing financial goals. Periodic adjustments ensure your budget remains effective and aligned with life changes and evolving priorities.

# Chapter 14: Budgeting and Investing Basics

1. Why is investing important, and how does it differ from saving?

Investing helps money grow over time through compound interest and market returns, while saving preserves money in low-risk, easily accessible accounts. Investing is essential for long-term goals, like retirement, because it offers potential growth that outpaces inflation, unlike savings, which may lose value due to rising prices.

2. How can I include investing in my budget?

Allocate a set percentage of your income (e.g., 10–20%) to investments based on your financial goals. Automating contributions to investment accounts after each paycheck makes investing consistent and ensures it's prioritized in your budget.

3. What's the difference between stocks, bonds, and mutual funds?

Stocks: Ownership shares in a company, offering high potential returns but also higher risk.
Bonds: Loans to companies or governments, providing more stable but lower returns.
Mutual Funds: Pooled investments in various assets (stocks, bonds), offering diversification and professional management. Each serves a different purpose, with stocks for growth and bonds for stability.

4. How do I decide how much risk to take with my investments?

Your risk tolerance depends on your age, financial goals, and time horizon. Younger investors with a longer timeline may take on more risk for growth (e.g., more stocks), while those nearing retirement might prefer conservative investments (e.g., bonds) to protect their savings.

5. What is a diversified portfolio, and why is it important?

A diversified portfolio spreads investments across different asset types (e.g., stocks, bonds, real estate) to reduce risk. This balances potential returns and protects against significant losses in any one area, creating a more stable path to financial growth.

6. How can I get started with investing if I don't have a lot of money?

Start with low-fee index funds, ETFs, or micro-investing platforms which allow small initial investments. Even small contributions, when made regularly, can grow over time through compounding.

7. What are index funds and ETFs, and why are they popular among beginners?

Index funds and ETFs track a specific market index (e.g., S&P 500), offering broad market exposure, diversification, and low fees. Their simplicity and cost-effectiveness make them ideal for beginners looking for steady, long-term growth.

8. How can I avoid common investing mistakes as a beginner?

Avoid trying to "time the market," making emotional investment decisions, and neglecting fees. Stick to a long-term strategy with regular contributions, be patient, and remember that compounding works best over time.

9. How do I monitor my investments without becoming overwhelmed?

To monitor your investments without becoming overwhelmed, set quarterly or semi-annual check-ins to review portfolio performance instead of checking daily. This long-term approach reduces stress and helps maintain a focus on overall progress rather than short-term market fluctuations.

10. How do I reinvest dividends, and why is it beneficial?

Dividends are payments from companies to shareholders, which can be reinvested to buy more shares. Reinvesting dividends allows for compounding growth, helping your investments grow faster over time.

11. What's the role of a financial advisor, and should I consider one?

A financial advisor provides personalized investment advice and financial planning. You can consider one if your financial goals are complex or if you need guidance, but for simpler needs, robo-advisors or self-management may be more cost-effective.

12. How does dollar-cost averaging work, and how can it reduce risk?

Dollar-cost averaging involves investing a fixed amount regularly, regardless of market conditions. This reduces the impact of market volatility by buying more shares when prices are low and fewer when prices are high, smoothing out returns over time.

13. How should I balance my investments with other financial goals, like debt repayment?

Prioritize high-interest debt repayment while contributing to retirement accounts, especially if your employer offers matching contributions. This approach allows you to reduce debt while benefiting from the growth potential of investments.

14. What is rebalancing, and how often should I do it?

Rebalancing is adjusting your portfolio to maintain your desired asset allocation (e.g., 60% stocks, 40% bonds) as market fluctuations shift the balance. Rebalance annually or semi-annually to stay aligned with your risk tolerance and financial goals.

# Chapter 15: Reflecting and Adjusting Your Budget Over Time

1. Why is it important to revisit my budget periodically?

Regular budget reviews are important because life circumstances, financial goals, and spending habits change over time. Revisiting your budget ensures it remains relevant and effective, helping you adapt to new priorities and stay on track with your financial goals.

2. How often should I review and adjust my budget?

A monthly review helps monitor spending and make small adjustments, while a more comprehensive quarterly or annual review assesses larger financial goals and life changes. Monthly check-ins keep things on track, and annual reviews ensure long-term alignment.

3. What signs indicate that my budget needs adjustment?

Signs that indicate that your budget needs adjustment include consistently overspending in certain categories, changes in income, unexpected expenses, or shifting financial goals. If you notice patterns of stress or financial strain, it's likely time to adjust your budget.

4. How do I adjust my budget after a significant life event, like a job change or move?

After major life events, reassess your income, expenses, and financial goals. Adjust budget categories to reflect any new responsibilities or opportunities. Budgeting is flexible, allowing you to adapt smoothly to life transitions.

5. How do I handle fluctuating income when adjusting my budget?

To handle fluctuating income when adjusting your budget, create a "base budget" that covers essential expenses with your lowest expected income. During higher-income months, build a buffer fund to cover shortfalls in leaner months. This strategy provides stability despite income fluctuations.

6. How can I keep my budget aligned with my long-term goals?

To keep your budget aligned with your long-term goals, periodically review your long-term goals and ensure your spending and saving habits support them. Set smaller, measurable milestones to track monthly or quarterly, keeping your larger financial objectives in focus.

7. How can I incorporate new financial goals into my budget?

To incorporate new financial goals into your budget, set clear, realistic savings targets for new goals. Reallocate funds from existing categories if needed, and adjust your budget to prioritize short-term goals with more aggressive saving, while gradually working on long-term objectives.

8. How can I use my past budgeting successes and failures to improve my future budget?

Reflect on past spending patterns to identify successful strategies and areas needing improvement. Use these insights to create a more realistic, personalized budget that aligns with your habits and financial priorities.

9. What role does tracking my net worth play in budget adjustments?

Tracking your net worth gives you a broader view of your financial health and progress toward financial independence. Use net worth updates as a motivator to adjust your budget for increased savings or debt reduction.

10. How do I handle "budget fatigue" if I feel worn out by tracking every expense?

Simplify your budget by focusing on high-impact categories and automating savings. Consider taking breaks from tracking small expenses or switching to broader methods like percentage-based budgeting to reduce burnout.

11. What's the best way to make budgeting a lifelong habit?

Consistency and adaptability can make budgeting a lifelong habit. View budgeting as a tool for reaching your goals rather than a restriction. Regular check-ins and occasional adjustments keep the process sustainable and aligned with your evolving needs.

12. How can I ensure my budget reflects my values and priorities over time?

Regularly reflect on your values and priorities, then adjust your budget to align with them. Ask yourself if your spending supports your desired lifestyle, and make changes as your values evolve.

13. How do I celebrate financial milestones while staying within my budget?

To celebrate financial milestones while staying within your budget, set aside a small "celebration fund" to reward yourself when you reach milestones without derailing your budget. Celebrating progress reinforces positive habits, making budgeting feel rewarding instead of restrictive.

# Conclusion

Congratulations on taking the first steps toward financial control and stability! Budgeting isn't about perfection, it's about progress, persistence, and personal growth. With the knowledge and tools you've gained, you're well-equipped to create a budget that supports your dreams, adapts to life's changes, and enables you to live life on your terms.

Remember, budgeting is your tool for success, and with each step, you're building a life of financial freedom and confidence. Adopt the process, celebrate your achievements, and stay committed to your financial journey.

www.ingramcontent.com/pod-product-compliance
Lightning Source LLC
Chambersburg PA
CBHW070705240526
45472CB00023B/1492